ANGELA LANSBURY

A detailed look at her Life, Movies, Awards, Death, Biography, & 7 Interesting things about her Life you might not have known

By
Christine G. Bryant

Table of Content

Chapter 1

How did Angela Lansbury Died? And what caused it?

As author Jessica Fletcher, an amateur detective on the television show "Murder, She Wrote" Lansbury, a five-time Tony Award winner and three-time Oscar contender, solved 12 seasons' worth of murders; this character earned her Emmy nominations each year, but she never won.

Between 1984 and 1996, the Sunday night program produced four TV movies. It was a rating success and followed America's most-watched news program, 60 Minutes; both shows attracted millions of intelligent and older audiences.

In addition, Lansbury was one of the select few female television actors to have her own series.

What was the reason for Angela Lansbury's passing and how did she die?

Her family announced that Lansbury passed away on October 11, 2022, at 1:30 a.m., as she was sleeping in her Los Angeles, California, home. Five days short of her 97th birthday, on October 11, 2022, at 1:30 a.m. at home in Los Angeles, according to her daughters, their mother passed away quietly in her sleep.

David Shaw, Lansbury's stepson; Anthony Shaw, her son; and Deirdre Shaw, her daughter, survive her. Lansbury had children with Peter Shaw, her second husband, whom she wed from 1949 until his death from a heart attack on January 29, 2003. Age-wise, he was 84. She is survived by her three children, Anthony, Deirdre, and David; her three grandsons, Peter, Katherine, and Ian; five great-grandchildren; and her brother, producer Edgar Lansbury. Peter Shaw, her husband of 53 years, preceded her in death.

What caused Angela Lansbury's passing?

According to Lansbury's relatives, she died naturally. 17 years had passed since Lansbury had knee replacement surgery in July 2005, during which the degenerating cartilage in her knee joint was replaced with metal and plastic. "People were assisting me in crossing the street, I discovered". In 2006, Lansbury told the East Bay Times that her early dancing profession had left her with "crippled" knees and that she had to "drag herself up the stairs." "I started to feel old, yet I still had a very youthful heart. I won't be participating in Dancing with the Stars at this time in my life", she said.

However, I want to move about and dance, so I did, and I can. She admitted to delaying the operation at the time to the East Bay Times out of concern that it would be too painful.

After having a hip replaced in May 1994, Lansbury had knee replacement surgery as well. A representative for Murder, She Wrote for CBS informed the Greensboro News & Record at the time, "She has experienced some hip issues, but not enough to affect her job." The moment she went on break, she realized that this was the right time to deal with it.

Additionally, Lansbury's death followed a protracted battle with arthritis, a condition for which she first displayed signs in the 1990s. After Lansbury missed "A tribute to her" at the 75th Annual Tony Awards in 2022, she reasoned that remaining at home was the wisest move since she was at a theater with 6,000 people and there were still frequent COVID instances.

Three months before her passing, Lansbury spoke on an interview and said that although she was still healthy, her arthritis forced her to give up interests like gardening. Athough she still enjoys things like cooking, reading, and doing crossword puzzles, it was difficult for her to keep her weight under control. I get adequate sleep and I take a lot of vitamins, she said. "I think becoming older shouldn't stop you from continuing. I am still here and moving forward, just like the waves.

Lansbury also said that she began smoking at the age of 14 and didn't stop until 30 years before she passed away in an interview in 2022. She said at the time that she had been smoking since she was truly about 14 years old: "I was able to pull a cigarette out of a package in my handbag and smoke it, something I hadn't been able to let on." "I say it with absolutely no feeling of pride. And thirty years ago, I gave up smoking. But even so, you may recall that I do smoke a fairly lengthy Cigarettello in the movie. And in the Gaslight movie, there was a component of commerce. I was just allowed to huff it, however. And, as Mr. Clinton would say, I wasn't permitted to breathe.

In a 2014 interview with The Daily Mail, Lansbury outlined the reasons she believed Murder, She Wrote was a hit. I see why Murder, She Wrote was a hit, she remarked. "There was never any violence or blood. A whodunnit's gratifying resolution was also present. The puzzle was finished. And I adored Jessica's portrayal of an average lady. That, in my opinion, is what made her so appealing to a broad audience.

For each season of Murder, She Wrote, Lansbury received an Emmy nomination for Outstanding Lead Actress in a Drama Series; yet, she never took home the prize. Lansbury discussed this in an interview with Radio Times in 2017. At that moment, she said, "It irritated me." "Because in Hollywood, I simply didn't add up at all. Murder, She Wrote was very popular everywhere else in the United States, but not in Hollywood — no, no, no, they didn't care. I wasn't upset, but in all honesty, I was. It bothered me. I'm unable to claim it didn't. Lansbury expressed her pride in the play to Star2 in 2018 despite not receiving any honors for it. It was a portion of her career that she stated had nothing to do with anything else she had previously done. It took me many years to develop Jessica Fletcher into the role I ultimately played. She was a little bit silly at first, but I eventually transformed her into a lady of my own age and intelligence. She was someone that people could relate to and integrate into their lives, and I believe that is what made her such an endearing figure in the world.

Chapter 2

Biography: Her life, Movies, & Awards

She was the daughter of Northern Irish actor Moyna Macgill and Edgar Lansbury, a socialist politician who was a councilor and mayor in the east London district of Poplar.

She was born in the Regent's Park area of London in 1925.

Even more prominent in left-leaning politics was her paternal grandfather, George Lansbury, who led the Labour party from 1932 to 1935. Even after moving to the United States, his granddaughter maintained a fascination with British politics, questioning English interviewers about the virtues of Wilson, Kinnock, Blair, and, later, Corbyn.

This passion was a way for her to honor her father, who passed away when she was only nine years old.

Her participation in school performances and subsequent training at dance and acting institutions helped her overcome the obstacles that plagued her upbringing.

When she was asked, in an interview celebrating her 90th birthday, what advice she would offer to young performers, it seemed to corroborate the impression that she considered performing to be an escape from the misery she had been experiencing.

In direct opposition to the conventional acting instruction that instructs performers to draw on their own emotional experiences while playing a part, she said, "Leave who you are at home... all that everyday stuff." If I allow my experiences to intrude on the lives and experiences of the character, I will be placing a barrier in front of myself that will prevent me from developing into someone completely different from the person that I am.

Acting had also been more like freedom for her throughout her youth when the Nazi bombardment of London in 1940 forced her mother to leave with her children for Canada and later the United States. During this time, she had been acting.

Angela, being a teenager, created a cabaret performance based on Noel Coward's songs while working there. She also performed little roles. At the age of 17, she met John Van Druten, who had written the script for

Gaslight, at a party that was held by her mother. She was offered a contract with MGM for seven years after being cast in it on his advice.

Lansbury's career in Hollywood was never nearly as successful as it seems it would be, despite the fact that she was nominated for an Oscar for both Gaslight and her subsequent picture, The Picture of Dorian Gray. This was in part because of her most famous film role, which was as the manipulative mother of a presidential assassin in the film "The Manchurian Candidate", which was released in 1962, was unavailable for public viewing for a considerable amount of time because of fears that the plot had predicted the assassination of President John F. Kennedy in 1963.

However, the disappointment of Hollywood was quickly offset by the renown of Broadway. Lansbury was a surprise choice for the main part of the eccentric socialite Mame in the musical Mame, which she played in 1966. The story takes place during the Great Depression. She was showered with praise and won her first Tony award for the part, but in another blow to her career, Lucille Ball was cast as Mame and earned negative reviews for her performance in the 1974 film adaptation of the play.

However, Lansbury went on to play a variety of Sondheim divas in revivals of Gypsy and A Little Night Music. She also created the role of the cannibalistic pie-maker, Mrs. Lovett, in Sweeney Todd (1979), for which she drew on her childhood memories to assume a plausible cockney accent.

In addition, Lansbury won an Academy Award for her performance in Sweeney Todd (1979).

Next, Lansbury demonstrated her mastery of a third performing craft by starring in the television series Murder, She Wrote (1984–1996). The program quickly became and continues to be one of the most successful television shows of all time. Lansbury played Jessica Fletcher, a writer, and detective.

It's possible that the network was concerned about having a woman who was over 60 anchoring a primetime program, and that's why, in the opening seconds of the first episode, Lansbury was shown first vigorously cycling, and then sprinting full-pelt to take a phone call.

In the first book of the series, titled "The Murder of Sherlock Holmes," a recently widowed journalist named Mrs. Fletcher watches a few moments of a whodunnit rehearsal in her hometown of Cabot Cove, New England, where she lives, and correctly identifies the perpetrator of the crime. She does this while volunteering at a local theater.

In the next scene, she finds out that one of her nephews has sold the mystery book that she has been writing as a pastime to a publisher behind her back. Her career as the best-selling crime writer J.B. Fletcher was launched with a sideline as an amateur sleuth, solving murders that occurred near her home or in other locations (New York, Los Angeles, Hawaii) to which she has gone on book tours or to speak at engagements.

Her books have been translated into several different languages.

Another respected long-timer, Jean Stapleton, had been offered the role before Lansbury's casting, but she declined the opportunity. The casting was yet another stroke of professional luck that accentuated Lansbury's career. Lansbury created the part a superb vehicle for the affable intellect and charming mischievousness that were the core components of her acting personality, and she did this by making the job a perfect fit for the character. For the role, she adopted a little more American accent, albeit she always spoke with an English accent off-screen during her whole life.

It might be said that Lansbury's second husband, Peter Shaw, and their son, Anthony, turned the production of Murder, She Wrote into something of a family enterprise, since both of them produced or directed several episodes.

Lansbury was unhappy when the show was canceled in 1996, seemingly because it was now seen as too cozy and too old, with the star having passed the age of 70. The demanding schedule of a US television hit led Lansbury to reduce her involvement at times; her character, Jessica, only appeared in the prologue and epilogue of some shows.

Cheekily, the last episode, number 264, was titled "Death by Demographics," and it had Mrs. Fletcher going to the help of a veteran radio books program presenter whose position was taken over by an uncouth shock jock.

Murder, She Wrote spawned a total of four TV movies that were spin-offs, and the program has had a fruitful afterlife thanks to syndication and repeated airings.

As audiences of television programs grew increasingly diverse, the presence of an older female main character began to be seen less as a disadvantage and more as an opportunity. Lansbury engaged in several fruitless endeavors to revive the program, but to no avail.

Lansbury had her last appearance on the London stage in 2014 when she was 88 years old. She played Madame Arcati, a dotty clairvoyant, in a production of Noel Coward's 1941 comedy Blithe Spirit.

The performance, which took place at the Gielgud Theatre on Shaftesbury Avenue in London, was perhaps the last one to include an actor who had been a leading light during Coward's time. Because Moyna Macgill made her acting debut there in 1915, the location provided Lansbury with a great deal of emotional joy because it was the same arena in which she had performed. Lansbury told an interviewer that she sensed the presence of her mother in the building, which may have been an appropriate comment given that the play was about seances.

"I think people such as her, who have been acting since they were teenagers, develop special gifts because they learn the basics of their craft when they are young and impressionable, she has a remarkable capacity for self-control. Maintains a very high level of physical fitness" Michael Blakemore, her director in Blithe Spirit, gushed to the Guardian in 2015 as the actor turned 90

She made a remarkable announcement that she would be returning to Broadway in the 2017 season, where she will star in a production of the 1955 drama The Chalk Garden by Enid Bagnold. Lansbury found it amusing that she was one of the few actors who would need to 'age down' to portray the role of Mrs. St. Maugham, an ancient matriarch.

However, as time went on, she began to question whether or not she could maintain the endurance necessary to play eight concerts each week.

At the age of 91, she gave her last performance on a New York stage, which was a one-night staged reading of The Chalk Garden at the theater of Hunter University. She did this as a sort of consolation for herself.

In the same year, she played Aunt March in a UK-US rendition of Little Women by Louisa May Alcott, and she conveyed the paradoxical severity and charm of the character with the characteristic accuracy that she is known for.

Angela Lansbury was without a doubt one of the most famous stage and film actresses in American history, and that iconic part she played seemed like the perfect way to say goodbye to television in every way except for the fact that it was her last television performance.

Chapter 3

7 interesting things about her life you might not have known

In "Beauty and the Beast," she provided the voice of Mrs. Potts.

"Cheer up child, it'll turn out all right in the end. You'll see."

In the Disney animated feature Beauty and the Beast, Lansbury provided her voice for Mrs. Potts, the role of everyone's favorite motherly teapot.

This implies that she was also the voice behind the entrancing theme song for the Disney classic from 1991.

She expressed her gratitude for her youthful audience by saying, "This was a breakthrough for me."

It introduced me to a generation that I probably wouldn't have been able to get in touch with otherwise.

She performed "Beauty and the Beast" at New York's Lincoln Center.

To commemorate the film's 25th anniversary and take the stage at New York's Lincoln Center, Lansbury delivered a mesmerizing performance of the main theme song while the audience was there in 2016.

She has a place in the Guinness World Records book in two different categories.

The most well-known detective in Cabot Cove has made it into the annals of history.

The fictitious figure is recognized by Guinness World Records as having the title of "Most Prolific Amateur Sleuth."

There is also a cameo appearance by Lansbury herself.

She took home the most Tony Awards for the role of Best Actress in a Musical, cementing her place in theater history.

Taking up the role of Aunt Adelaide in She was dragged "up from the depths" by Nanny McPhee.

In 2003, Lansbury's spouse passed away due to complications from heart failure.

Two years later, she played the role of Aunt Adelaide in the critically acclaimed children's film Nanny McPhee.

After the death of her husband, Lansbury was quoted as saying in an interview that her work on the television show Nanny McPhee "pulled me out of the abyss."

She was a star in the production of Driving Miss Daisy which was staged in Australia.

Driving Miss Daisy, a play written in 1987 that was awarded the Pulitzer Prize, was staged in Australia in 2013, and Angela Lansbury starred in the lead role.

She played the role of Miss Daisy Werthan, a Jewish grandmother of 72 years who is recently widowed and is told by her son that she is too old to drive.

James Earl Jones, who played Daisy's chauffeur, also starred in the film alongside Angela Lansbury.

She was a Turnbull family member and Malcolm's cousin.

Angela Lansbury and the late former Prime Minister of Australia Malcolm Turnbull are related, as was revealed by Turnbull on his twitter page. The politician, who is 67 years old, paid tribute to Lansbury.

Mr. Turnbull posted a photo of him and her together in 2013 when she was performing Driving Miss Daisy in Sydney. He referred to her as "Aunty Angela" in the caption of the photo.

She had a role in one of the Mary Poppins sequels.

Lansbury had a brief but memorable appearance in the feature film Mary Poppins Return, which was released in 2018 and is a sequel to the original film, which was released in 1964.

Lansbury portrays an elderly lady who brings pleasure to people during the Great Depression by selling balloons in a park where she works. The story takes place in London 20 years later, at the time of the Great Depression.

Made in the USA
Las Vegas, NV
04 February 2024

85289979R00017